RHYMES

'N

RHYTHMS

'N

BLUES

M. Nannette Marchand

RHYMES 'N RHYTHMS 'N BLUES

Cover Design and Book Layout by
Poncho Williams/PDUB Graphics

Photo by Erika Kinniebrew

dedication

i dedicate this book to my family, the Marchands, the Merritts and the Mabins. These three remarkable pillars continue to inspire, encourage and support my writing. It is also dedicated to my dearest friends who routinely embolden my creative spirit and reinforce my imagination.

acknowledgements

Thank you, Deberon, Tom, Michele, and Dom;
you are the family treasures whose unconditional love
and advocacy nurture my muses.

Thank you, Crystal, your friend/mentorship and
guidance has kept me centered and held me
steadfast to honing my craft.

Judie, Marcia, Kaärren and Pat, I am grateful for your
encouragement; you continue to feed my spirit with
your amazing sisterlove.

Poncho, thank you for coupling your exceptional
artistic talents with your masterful musicianship
to create a cover that invites the reader in to
explore an objet d'art.

contents

rhymes

contents

rhythms

contents

blues

Low Notes

Mental Notes

Blue Notes

contents

pilogue

RHYMES

love notes

Moments

Upon waking

    you enter my mind

You are welcome

    I find

myself reliving,

    recounting each moment,

that we

    Combed our minds free ---

and

you lent

me your cherished thoughts on music

Discovering similar notes

sounding euphonic

Moments that

were, are and will be

bright, shy, shared

JEWELS

Jewels and gems
precious and few
Rough, uncut
yet. . .brilliant in hue

Sheathed in rock
covered in earth
clever disguises
shield your worth

Glistening glimmers
wrapped in rust
gold and silver
peek through dust

Chromatic stones
catch the sun's rays
then play hide n' seek
'til the end of the day

Fashioned by waves
and grains of sand
a shimmering pearl
comes to rest on land

Treasured jewels
are words sometimes,
whether in song or
prose or rhyme

True delicate jewels
are handled with care
---they're genuine friendships
but oh, so rare

THE COMFORT ZONE OF LOVE

You thought it would be easy
when we parted friends
you said you wanted space
to be free again

Your freedom kept you busy
I saw others too
you realized you missed me
I noticed I missed you

The comfort zone of love
was fashioned from our hearts
not something that we worked at
just natural from the start

Your body speaks a language
that I learned long ago
we understand each other
our love can only grow

Open to our feelings
acknowledging respect
the comfort zone of love
was easy to accept

MY HEART WASN'T FREE

My heart wasn't free
    back when we first met
and you said,
    'let's be friends instead'
I never will forget...

The way you tiptoed 'round my heart
    so careful not to tread
inside that tangled web of fear
    the boundaries that we set

My heart wasn't free
    I mistook lust for love
and you said,
    'love is in your heart
not found in the bed'

So easily our friendship grew
    both learning how to trust
the fragile nature of new love
    and how our souls are fed

My heart wasn't free
    held captive by my thoughts
and you said,
    'I'll rescue your heart
and you'll have no regrets'

Love affairs may come and go
  a true friend stands with you
sharing good times, sometimes bad
    it was the friend you always knew

Brown Eyes

Love caught me by surprise
and gently carried me
I held the glance of Brown Eyes
I felt our thoughts run free

We shared a smile, breathed a sigh,
 created memories
I held the glance of Brown Eyes
I saw great mystery

'Tis often said we fantasize
While wading through life's stream
I held the glance of Brown Eyes
And wandered into a dream

ENHANCE MY MIND

Lightly you tap the well of my

Being

Thoughts float to the surface untouched

by fluoride

I feel the ladle as it gently dips

Carefully you sip

my words tasting sweet, fresh. . .

clinging like bits of moisture

to your lips

My insides, sometimes, feel dry

Lightly you tap the well of my

Being

creative instincts trickle down my

mind Into pools of lasting reflections

Only to tickle our souls

BEGINNINGS

Unexpected
Unannounced
deliberate and
pronounced

love swept in
with a fury
we decided
not to worry

though uncommon
it may be
to love
so desperately

in our hearts
there was no doubt
that neither one
could do without

the other
rather than deny
we chose to
recognize
the
familiar

you always knew me
but not my name
I always loved you
but waited 'til you came

WONDER

Wonder if. . .

he can see

that

I am ME

that

he is HE

that

HE and ME

could be WE?

playful notes

mystery

you're a mystery causin' me misery
a puzzle causin' me pain
I'd rather figure geometry
with nothin' to lose or gain

I've tried to find solutions
but only find a wall
I end up in confusion
with no answers at all

Why must you stay a mystery
behind that sheltered smile?
Hiding must get weary
won't you come out for a while?

It's certain that I love you
though a puzzle you may be
but could I not think of you
there'd be no mystery

BASKETBALL LOVE
(In the Court of My Mind and the Hoop of My Heart)

The pace is often frenzied

dashing to and fro

My heart is in the lead

I count your field goals.

While watching your gyrations

to score those winning points

There seems no limitation

to your limber joints.

The court withstands the pressure

my heart applauds your steps

you've brought inexhaustible pleasure

BECAUSE,

in your sneakers, into my heart,

you crept.

RIGHTEOUS ROOKIE

Everyday one enters
into the game of life
a neophyte, a rookie
to share in joy and strife

Whether one is punting
or running bases round
the quest may seem quite easy
but obstacles are found

true, everyone is different
and no one stays the same
yet rules and regulations
still unchanged, remain

scramble for position,
execute the "D",
be a sport, play fair life's game
for a pro was once a rookie

Suddenly You're There!

Grover blends his notes so rare
to "Bright Moments"...then
Suddenly, you're there!

Taj softly swears
"I'm Satisfied, Tickled Too"...then
Suddenly, you're there!

Angie swooned
"How hard I tried, how much I cared"...then
Suddenly, you're there!

The TV shouts CJs Jeeps
Need little repair...then
Suddenly, you're there!

Little brown 280Z's
parade up and down the thoroughfares...then
Suddenly, you're there!

Shamelessly I watch fights on TV...then
I stop and stare, and
Suddenly, you're there!

soft notes

MUSIC SOOTHES MY SOUL

As hope may calm someone's fears
As mothers quiet baby's tears
Music soothes my soul
And lets me know
that soft notes
caress like tender hands
When I don't have a man
to hold
Music soothes my soul

As sun peaks through a cloud of storm
As one seeks peace in early morn
Music soothes my soul
And lets me know
melody and harmony
are close friends
with whom I spend
happiness and woe
Music soothes my soul

As time heals a lover's wound
As two hearts gently hum a tune
Music soothes my soul
And lets me know
that loneliness is
just a word
While sounds blend sweet
and songs are heard
Music soothes my soul

Release My Soul

Writing doth release my soul
so heavenly the feelings flow
and life is captured with a pen
only to begin again – and again

and

Writing doth relieve me so
refreshing as a morning snow
delightful times, some sad, I know;
the paper shares my memories though.

While writing, poetry happened in
now we're cherished life-long friends
it's funny how words come and go.
Oh, how writing doth release my soul.

TOMORROW IS NOT PROMISED TO YOU (anyone)

If time were but the space

we view between the lines

there would not be

a guarantee

that we would be

Tomorrow is not a promise

nor is each breath we take

so live we must

with   dreams,   faults,   trust.

Unused moments turn to dust.

Dreams Belong To Dreamers

My dreams were stolen from me
...just lifted from my heart I
don't know who to turn to
...don't know where to start.

Stolen dreams, like heartaches
...sometimes sting the soul
but now I know the thief
has only made me whole.

I've learned...
No one takes another's dreams
...they borrow from the heart.
Dreams belong to dreamers
and they will never part.

REFLECTIONS

Reflections I shall always see
As long as time envelops me
would be:

      the beauty of
      the precious sun
      the welcome dusk
      (when day is done)
      the biting breeze
      of Winter's wind
      and then...
      Spring peeks through
      in pastel shades
      each fragrant blossom
      uniquely made
      Summer tiptoes behind spring
      laughing, teasing
      beaches, brown bodies, fireflies
      some say, "summer madness"
      happens by

Reflections guide this flowing mind
and every chance I get, I find
myself wandering through a kind
of place where thoughts and times
reach out in rhyme

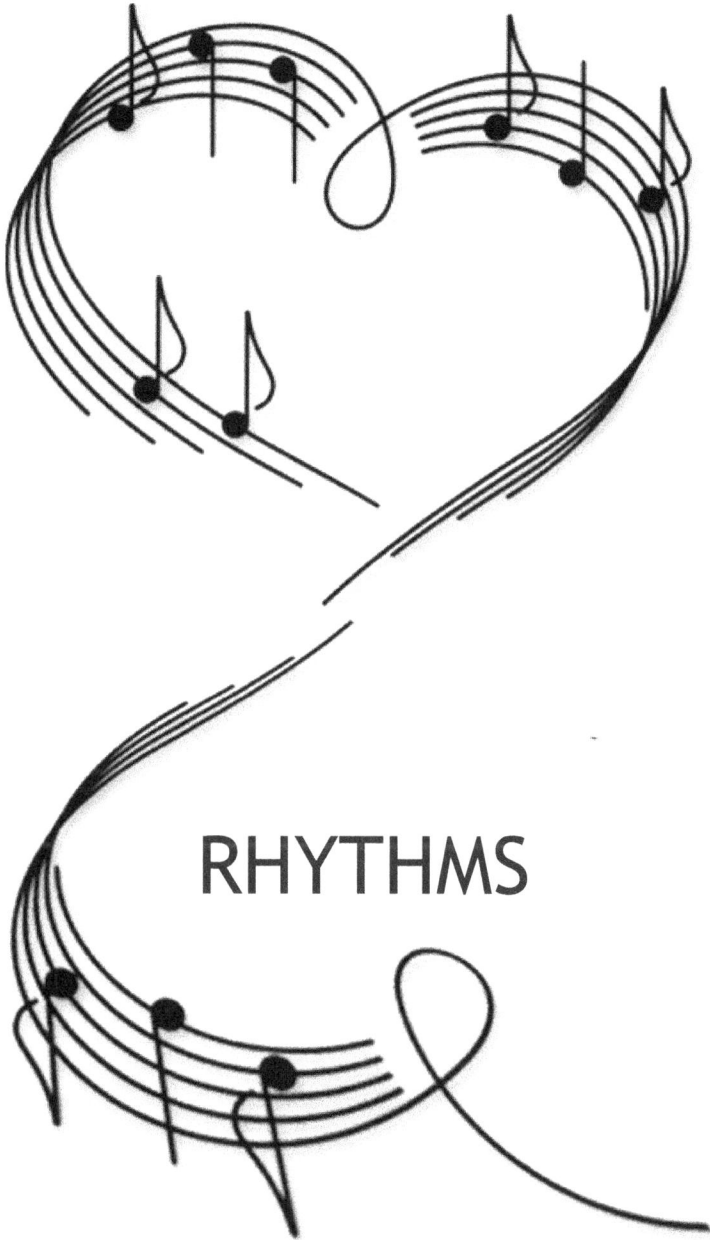

RHYTHMS

sensual notes

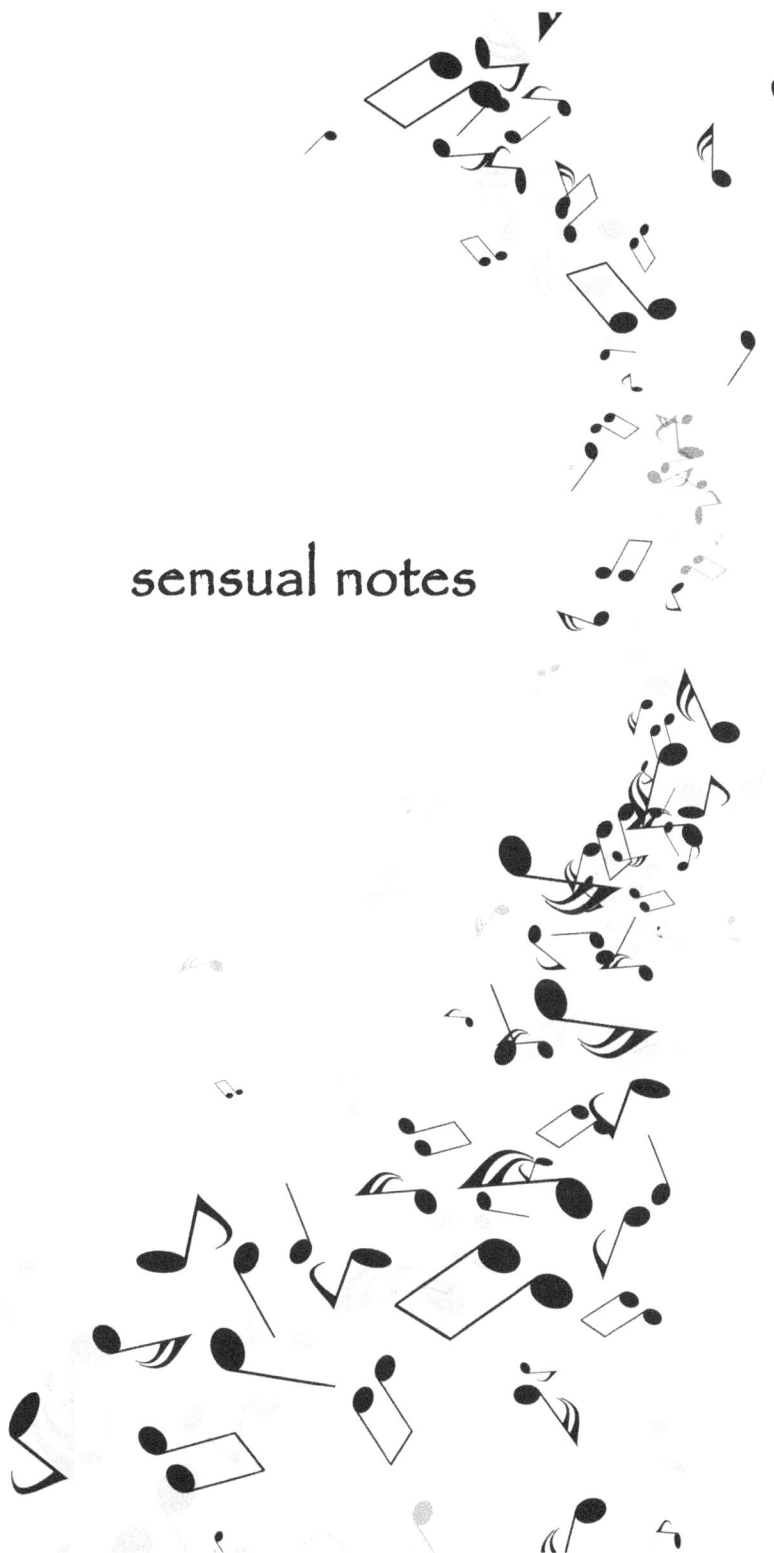

Untitled

Thought of you today

Have not heard

not EVEN word.

poured a glass of wine...

lit a candle...

wished for you today, everyday

tried to think of how you felt, mmm..mm

Soft rich brown skin

those lovable lips

that wonderful grin

and those strong, strong hips

YOU AGAIN

Oh I will have you to love and love
me

...and I will love you 'til you cain't be
loved no more

...and get angry with YOU over OUR actions,
sometimes words

...then...love you again

Almost...like...as if love stepped from a
crowded room, briefly --- only to return refreshed
with a romantic, infectious aroma

...know that, the connecting thread wound
round and round those pounding passions,
known as hearts, is unable to loose
itself

...and challenge your love, my security
because I'm human

...and question my love, your security
because you're human

...admit that our humanness overrules
the insecurities

...recognize the now moments and knowing the
risks --- SEIZE them with the EASE
that belongs to US

ENTER YOU. ENTER ME.
ENTER RISKS.

Oh yes, you will love me, be loved, and love being
loved by me

Except. . .Accept

Except for times like

these

I find it rude

that he intrudes

upon my solitude

Yet thoughts of him begin to

tease

and settle in

with natural ease

so, I

Accept times like

these

IN THE MIDDLE OF A DREAM

i hear you

in the middle of a dream

it seems

that you are here

that you are near

me

the voice is clear

soft, penetrating

SO GOOD, SO GOOD

i welcome the interruption

a sound so mystical, magical

and yet it's so

natural to

COME

in the middle of a dream

EARTH'S DESIGN

The earth's design
had you in mind...
your unique touch
adds so much
to what is there.

You are rare.

Though shrewd and
sometimes lewd,
the magnetism still exudes

The above may seem untrue
BUT
As seen by one
This is you

lyrical notes

TELL ME.

Tell me.

What's wrong with loving you?
accept my love as something new
give me some, some love from you
need me, want me, love me too

Just because you're not here
don't think my love will disappear
moments spent with you are dear
kiss me, stroke me, hold me near

Love, Sweet Love, don't run from me
You seem frightened, can that be?
loving you makes me feel free
take me, touch me, reach for me

One Moment of Your Love

One moment of your love
will keep me going strong
Let's make this moment many
Let's make it last so long

We sense each other's feelings
two hearts can't be wrong
Let's make this moment many
Let's make it last so long

Our hearts found harmony
let love create our song
Let's make this moment many
Let's make it last so long

If time were but one moment
we'll love on and on
Let's make this moment many
Let's make it last so – o – o l – o – n – g

WHEN YOUR BODY SPEAKS TO ME

When your body speaks to me
so soft, so tenderly
Your eyes suggest
a place to rest
I willingly agree

When your body speaks to me
no words are said by you
Yet with your kiss
I can't resist
the lovin' that we do

When your body speaks to me
you move so naturally
The way you dance
gives me a chance
to feel you close to me

BRIDGE   When your body speaks to me
You let your fingertips
Find the secret paths
Where you place your lips

When your body speaks to me
I hear your heartbeat too
Mine beats in syncopation
My heart will answer you

LOVE IS THE ANSWER

Love is the answer
...got somethin' to say
I'm not leavin'
I'm here to stay...

Stay with you
'til the end of time
love me, touch me
oh love of mine

Got me feelin'
all quick, then slow
It's your love, baby
that makes me glow

Yes. Love is the answer
to loneliness - desire
I've got plenty love, baby
set me on fire

BRIDGE   Love, Love, Love is the answer
Glide me, Love
Like a sweet slow dancer

I'LL NEVER WANT FOR LOVE AGAIN

Remembering when first we met

our eyes held fast, (please) don't <u>ever</u> let

me go too far away from him

I'll never want for love again

Thoughts of you take up my time

but I don't really seem to mind

We shared what could have, might have been

I'll never want for love again

I won't release my thoughts of you

So easily our friendship grew

then love, so quietly stepped in

I know, I'll never want for love again

I feel your love when you're not there

your touch, your smile, the way you care

You stay inside me, deep within

I'll never want for love again

TIME TAUGHT US

Time began to pass us by
and we began to wonder why
The answer stood before us
Blend our voices! Sing a chorus!

A love for music, we both shared
with heart and soul, we both dared
to sing songs of love and pain
we often laughed, sometimes complained

Something caught us by our souls
wouldn't let loose, revealed our goals
We held notes, held fast to words
Time taught us – be seen, be HEARD

Time taught us, taught us well
Take a chance, release the spell
one that keeps you down and out
take a chance, remove the doubt

BRIDGE   Time taught us...
                it's alright to take a chance
                We thought that...
                we were lost in a trance
                Time said believe...
                said reach for the moon
                We landed on a moonbeam that
                carried our tunes

THE
GAME
OF
FAME

Fame caught my eye
then headed for the door
I started singing
the applause cried, "MORE!"

Fame came by and
whispered in my ear
taunted and teased me
Never came near

They all came by
all famous in name
I stayed close
still searching for fame

BRIDGE The game of fame
can wear you out
you must know when
to trust, to doubt

Fame was a star-maker
for some, you see
Fame can be a heartbreaker
won't set you free

Lift Me

It seems life's been so unkind
but from day to day I find
the life we shared was not in vain
and though you're gone, I know I've gained

An understanding of our love that
reaches heights so far above
the physical needs we satisfied
like sharing joy; sometimes we cried

Our love combined, a child was born and
notes fell sweetly from your horn.
We loved, we learned, the moments we stole
Yes, all this and more strengthens my soul

Reaching out, I touch the bed
feeling where you laid your head
But I'll get by on memories
dreamin' dreams and fantasies

BRIDGE Lift me up, like you used to do
Lift me higher, don't want to be blue
Lift my spirits, oh do inspire
Lift me, lift me, higher - higher

high notes

STAY WOKE

Stay woke
and wipe your eyes
of residue
from wretched lies
Stay woke
and flush your ears
of bigoted sounds
from yesteryear
Stay woke
and cleanse your nose
to free the path
for fragrant prose
Stay woke
and clear your throat
to savor the victory
of your vote
Stay woke
and stay engaged
the fight for justice
is the war we wage

SOMEBODY

Somebody tell me now
Are we together here
or are we looking
past the visions that are near?

Somebody tell me now
Can we pretend today
is just the same
as yesterday...and hope
Tomorrow brings a change?

Somebody tell me now
If change is brought
by time
Can we afford
to have one day
to rest our minds?

Somebody tell me now
Is there a time and
place to be
and if we find this space
Will we all be free?

WHO'S TO SAY?

Who's to say

the reason why

things go awry

with those who try?

Who's to say

the way things go

that feeling low

will help one grow?

Who's to say

what's right or wrong

if short or long

what's weak or strong?

Who's to say

and understand

all that can

be done by man?

A COMEDY SITUATION

Laugh, smile, hullaboo

there's a chuckle to be found

No matter where you go,

look, listen to the subtle guffaws---

hee-hee.

The smiles are all around

sometimes well-hidden behind instant

camouflages producing the sound

of hushed giggles.

From day to day personalities merge

into a vaudevillian act creating

eight full hours of non-stop entertainment;

the comics come forth one at a time

to amuse the world from 8:15 to 4:45

sharp notes

YOU SHOULDA LOVED ME WHEN I LOVED YOU

It seems so strange not to love you
we've gone our separate ways
I've rearranged my feelings
Never thought I'd stay away

You found what you were looking for
she made your life so blue
Now you want to restore
the love I had for you
Well, it's too late
'cause I've found someone new

Nothin' you do will change my mind
you missed your chance to love
Someone else takes up my time
it's him that I dream of
Now I know how it feels
that my love is just enough

This time you say your love is real
you couldn't love before
Remember how you couldn't feel
and often closed the door?
When love found me, my spirits grew
and loving means much more

BRIDGE   You shoulda loved me
when I loved you
Life's too short to wait
You had my love within your reach
And now it is too late

Your shoulda loved me
when I loved you
Lovin' you was easy then
Now you know when you lose
You can't go back again

You shoulda loved me
when I loved you
It coulda been so sweet
You said you weren't quite ready
Now your life is incomplete

Have a good life, baby
And maybe, just maybe
You'll learn to love
When someone's lovin' you

IN MY MIND'S EYE

In my mind's eye
I see your face so clear
but when my eyes are open
you are so far yet near

the fragrance of the scent you wear
your coffee cup half-full
reminds me of the night we spent
no games were played, no rules

In my mind's eye
the vision is so real
the kiss you placed upon my lips
the tenderness I feel

the message you left on the phone
remains within my touch
your voice melodic, soothing
it relieves so much

In my mind's eye
I feel confident – secure
But when we are together
I'm not really sure

If deep down inside your heart
you feel the way I do
Do you frighten easily?
Are words you whisper, true?

In my mind's eye
I see a gentle soul
one who is responsive
--one I've rarely known

The prospect of complete love
is often tossed aside
but if our hearts are willing
'tis loving to have tried

DO YOU

1. Do you think?

    I do.

2. Do you think of. . .

    I do.

3. Do you think of good. . .

    I do.

4. Do you think of good times. . .

    I do.

5. Do you think of good times that. . .

    I do.

6. Do you think of good times that we've. . .

    I do.

7. Do you think of good times that we've shared together?

    Rarely do I.

BLUES

low notes

D
  E
    P
      R
        E
          S
            S

What a drag
              O
Running into snags
                S
smiling faces loom

like leers

Words pierce

my sensitive ears

Seems 'life's a bitch'

so unkind. . .which

makes me feel at times

so-o-o unnecessary and I'm

so inclined

to crawl

inside my wall

made from hopes of non-survival

but always surviving w
          i
         t
          h
            o
            u
             t
               a
                h
                 o
                  p
                   e...

73

HOW DOES FREEDOM RING?

ping . . . clink . . . chime

The ring of freedom is not loud
The noise is muted by a shroud
That does not ring true nor
proud

The sound is lowly, unheard
on high
One can't hear a bell once
it's died
Their deaths significant of living
a lie
That's not to say, the living <u>can</u>
hear
The so-called "sound" when all is
clear
Nor does it matter how near the
ear

The question, then, is simply posed:
    "How does freedom ring?"
The answer, one could suppose:
        "Ding-a-ling-a-ling."

LONG GREEN BLUES

Apparently one needs cash

to survive

the scheme of things

to stay alive

and well. . .

balance the checkbook

pay on time

keep good credit

sign your name

on the dotted line

BEWARE ☠

You may owe your very soul

if captured in the

snare of debt---well I

DECLARE!

bankruptcy if you must

after all, the SYSTEM IS JUST. . .

isn't it?

SOMEWAY, SOMEHOW

Someway, Somehow I've **Got** to

Pull through this

ORDEAL

But is it real?

Am I

living a lie

or will truth shine

and clear my mind

of these useless thoughts

And rhymes?

It's hard to say

in terms of time.

Time is space, I understand;

so space is time, on the other hand.

   Solutions don't come easy

that's plain to me

eventually (undefined time)

the answers will arrive

unexpected – but welcome

and by some

stroke of luck

I'll no longer be stuck

in this indecisive muck

MELANCHOLIA

No deposit, no return
  is often how I feel
and then I start to wonder
  am I even real?

my soul is somewhat empty my
mind seems hollow too
can love drink dry my spirits
  and color life so blue?

Discard cans and bottles;
Their usefulness complete
can love for one another
  be thrown away so neat?

REST FROM ROMANCE

Taking a rest from romance

Taking a leave from love

I never thought I'd see the day

BUT thank the Lord Above

I finally found that feeling

That frees me through and through

I'm taking that REST from ROMANCE

I'm taking a REST from you.

mental notes

WHAT OF TOMORROW?

I was struck by what I read

i n t o the headlines,

'cause it said:

APARTHEID LIVES –

BUT LIVES ARE DEAD

Forced to abandon dignity, hope

nothing left to borrow –

babies die, mothers cry

'what of tomorrow?"

Inflicting pain on

body and brain

so filled my soul with horror

then freedom fed

me as I read ...

wryly, I said,

"what of tomorrow?"

Oppressors will one day be

the OPPRESSED and – OH WHAT SORROW!

for they too will ask

"what of tomorrow?"

Who Knows

What's it all about?

Alfie didn't know

The clichés come and go

   "What's happenin?"

   "What it is?"

   "What's up?"

   "What's goin' on?"

The hip, the Unhip dote

on these words said by rote

not waiting for replies

just handing out more jive

asiftosay

I KNOW

Alfie didn't know

CIRCUMSTANCES

Circumstances beyond our

Control

Fuzzy, hazy, so many distortions

Turn the knobs this way

and that

Give it a shake, then a pat

No need to get uptight

'Things'll work out right' (they say)

Technical difficulties

beyond our control

Taken on by the experts

as they tease and cajole

the technological mind

made of vessels and veins

of all colors and kinds

Push the buttons, turn the dials

Can our minds

withstand the trials?

Sometimes the victim (often the volunteer)

of extenuating circumstances

so we take our chances

Seemingly innocent of the charge that

we are not in control

but actually guilty of governing

the whole.

WHY

are we all so
caught up in ourselves
to think we know
the answers, so much so,
that we won't delve
further and ask 'why?'

Can our beings be
so-o
TOGETHER
that **WE**
have no further
to go?

I hardly think so.

Be bold.

Pose the question 'why?'
and feel the tremors unearth
questions, questions and more
questions.
REALIZE that **EVERYTHING IS NOT
KNOWN
BY YOU**
some things you **THINK**
are true

ARE NOT.

Ask 'why?' to know,
to see **BEYOND** what
your eyes behold,
to **BE** whole.

blue notes

IN A HURRY TO DIE

Come and go
go and come
and so it goes
with everyone
who must be
at the stroke
of three
in the car
driving near
or far/
and so it goes
the freeways
JAMMED
with howling
kids
and "I'll be
damneds"
as uttered by
the irate kind
who have no time
to sit
and wait
heaven forbid!
should THEY
be late
while others
merely breathe
a sigh

---PATIENT---

not in a
hurry
to die

BEYOND TEARS

Years and Years and Years
have summoned me to their side
now, I'm beyond tears…
nothin' to hide

Will someone ever be here
to share my old and new
now that I'm beyond tears…
nothin' but blue

Along with pain and fear
I'll continue my façade
now that I'm beyond tears
will I sing or shout or s
             o
               b

DEPARTURE

It seemed to us, his hopes took flight
despair came in its place
and all the damage that was
done was written on his face. . .

And so, our thoughts are
somewhat empty now
Our hearts seem hollow too
We think, how can life be so
unkind and color love so blue?

But we'll remember joyous times
and cherish them each dawn
nothing can erase our love
just because he's gone.

WANDER

How long must one

wander through

life and times

and life and times

before one finds:

      the ties that bind

      a love so kind

      some peace of mind

      and peace?

Seemingly, such a search

might yield:

      that the key

      to being free

      may cost a fee:

      one's life and times

MURDER8

It's accepted
and expected
the MURDER8
will rise...
it comes as no surprise
that Inglewood has,
JAN 2014
8 homicides.
Guns in
brown n' black hands
of those
roaming land
claiming streets
in combat gear
ready to strike
show no fear
no remorse
shoot to kill
life is cheap
shoot to thrill.
Nervous cops
seem constrained
don't know how to
stop the train.
The collective cry
in all neighborhoods
STOP THE MURDERS
IN INGLEWOOD!

LONGING

i become very vulnerable

in night's dark recesses

i fool myself into thinking

i'm loved

but in dawn's early light

i know i'm alone

La Fin

i know now. . .

i am truly unafraid. . .

to die a natural death

We interrupt your

regularly scheduled

body functions. . .

for expiration purposes.

PERMANENT CANCELLATION OF PROGRAMMING

When she tried
. . .no one heard
then she died
. . .not a word
everyone cried
. . .it was absurd

EPILOGUE

Notes

from

One Weary Negress

ODE TO OBAMA

I heard the words
Change

Hope

Audacity

a New path

for Growth

and Evolution in America

You listened to the
Cries

for Help,

the expressions of Anger

Never losing sight

of the Goals

for a better Earthdom

I heard the call to join
the Cause

to make good things Happen

in this world Aware of living

In the Now

and recognizing Greatness

through our own Eyes

You listened to the
Creativity

of Humanity and

summoned the spirit of Angels

sitting Next to

God watching

over Everyone

You listened and heard
the Call to serve

with Humility,

Authenticity,

Nobility

and the Generosity of your Soul.

We Exhale with a global heartbeat.

BROTHER LOVE

From early on
you made up your mind
to always help others
to always be kind

When you were just five
your teacher told Mom
you placed all the books
just where they belonged

Your Lionel trains
were a sight to behold
we knew not to touch
without being told

Tinkering with bikes
was your next specialty
you made the old ones new
and mastered the "wheelie"

Forging friendships as a teen
you were a magnet strong
the bonds formed were unbreakable
The GR Posse --- lifelong

You polished your skills set
reached monumental heights
perfected your knowledge
to mega-giga bytes

You troubleshoot our cars,
our TVs, and our phones
not to mention our computers
you unturn every stone

We love you, Tommy Jr.
our Personal Tech Guru
your expertise --- a goldmine
your humor is special too

Suffice it to say, dear brother
we're proud to be your sibs
we've known your generous heart
since we were kids!

SUNFLOWER

SUNSHINE PEEKS
THROUGH CORNERS BRIGHT
YELLOW PETALS REACH
FOR THE LIGHT

FUZZY BROWN FACES
SMILE, BEND AND SWAY
BOWING, NODDING
GREETING THE DAY

GOD'S DESIGN
WITH PERFECT STEMS
FLANKED WITH LEAVES
SUPPORTING THEM

SLENDER FINGERS
TOUCHED BY GRACE
GROOM THIS GARDEN
AT A LOVING PACE

BUTTERFLIES 'N WINDCHIMES
WHISPER SWEET TUNES
'VERA, VERA
COME BACK SOON'

THE NAME VERA
IS TRUTH TO SOME
VERA ALSO MEANS FAITH
SHE WORE BOTH AS ONE

VERA'S GENEROUS SPIRIT
ENVELOPED EVERYONE
LIKE SUNFLOWERS, SHE GATHERED OUR HEARTS
AND FACED US TOWARD THE SUN

BLACK MEN, BLACK MEN

Black men, Black men, where are you?
You say you have to run
from the changes
WE put you through

Black men, Black men what do you see?
The whites in your eyes
cloud with trash and debris

Black men, Black men, you say
WE 'don't act right'
'cept when we give it up
we're better than white

Black men, Black men, don't you know
what to do?
Reach for BLACK WOMEN
all different – yet one
Our pride outweighs the heartbreak
of seeing you on the run

Black men, Black men, if you tire of running
your race against race
It may be too late
to pull from last place

Listen, Black men, WE know that we're strong
WE know that we're bright
How long must it be for you
to recognize that
ALL THAT GLITTERS AIN'T WHITE?

SHADES OF BLACK BEAUTY

Butterscotch, caramel, coffee, cream
Cocoa brown, chocolate
Rich ebony
Faces carved with African traits
Give testimony
To the African-American, the Motherland
Great
With sculpted strong shoulders
She carries the weight
Stepping so even walking so straight.

Royal tribesman, warriors shaped
Our history
Cornrows, braids, naturals adorned
Our heritage.
Textures of hair run the spectrum
Of unique
Bearing witness to our past, it is that
Pride we seek

The beauty found in blackness is not
Often told
blue-eyed images cloud perceptions
We hold
Creating confusion as features unfold
Full lips, rounded hips, broad noses
altered by some
to look more mainstream

has the majority won?

Dark is our continent
Swathed in colors bright
Legacies of ancestors give insight
To our Shades of Black Beauty.
Hues blend and find
They're steeped in tradition of
Body and Mind.

THE BEAUTY OF A LEGACY
(KUJICHAGULIA=Self-Determination)

O Motherland Great, hear us today
We honor your spirit, your wisdom, your ways

Abruptly your children were wrenched from your womb...
and reduced to a trade for golden doubloons

Packed in a vessel like fish caught from the sea
Some jumped overboard to meet their destiny

Forced into slavery, no shoes - shirts or belts
Instead they wore branches that grew from their welts

Forbidden to read, they did so at night and
stole away north with Moses by moonlight

Singing God's praises through hymnals and such
they created a code that kept them in touch

Even though beaten, molested, denied
their fierce self-determination could not be defied

O Ancestors brave, our heroines and heroes
We'll pass on our culture so everyone knows
The beauty of our legacy, a heritage sublime
As griots wise, perhaps an adage told in time

Self-Determination is not merely a hyphenated word
It's the freedom to choose
and the right to be heard.

ABOUT THE AUTHOR

M. Nannette Marchand refers to her style of writing as a poet and author who is on an interrupted continuum. While working as a Photo Research Analyst at Harcourt-Brace Jovanovich Publishing, she fashioned herself a music critic and submitted unsolicited reviews to Rolling Stone Magazine, covering performances throughout the Bay Area's fertile music scene.

Ms. Marchand met Grammy Award winning lyricist, arranger and producer, Skip Scarborough (Earth, Wind & Fire, Bill Withers, LTD, Anita Baker) and shared a copy of her first poem with him. Duly impressed, Scarborough insisted on placing it on the cover of his latest album project "Feel the Heat" featuring percussionist Bill Summers. The recording label rejected his efforts, so her poem "Moments" graced the inside cover of the album (aka sleeve). That incredible moment launched her path to poetry.

Her writing career led her to unlikely roads: volumes of poetry; author of WING TIPS, the autobiography of Tuskegee Airman Captain Claude C. Davis; sentiments/verses on greeting card lines; worked with Scarborough on numerous studio projects; assisted Herbie Hancock with his start-up interactive video enterprise, Hancock & Joe; created poems/tributes for numerous community/special events and served her city as a Police Commissioner.

In RHYMES 'N RHYTHMS 'N BLUES, Ms. Marchand offers a fascinating medley of melodic sensations, wry sensibilities while she lays down her burdens in the blues.

the end

www.ingramcontent.com/pod-product-compliance
Lightning Source LLC
Chambersburg PA
CBHW071146090426
42736CB00012B/2243